WHO WILL LOVE THE CROW

MIRIAM DUNN

This publication is a creative work protected in full by all applicable copyright laws, as well as by misappropriation, trade secret, unfair competition, and other applicable laws. No part of this book may be reproduced or transmitted in any manner without written permission from Winter Goose Publishing, except in the case of brief quotations embodied in critical articles or reviews. All rights reserved.

Winter Goose Publishing
45 Lafayette Road #114
North Hampton, NH 03862

www.wintergoosepublishing.com
Contact Information: info@wintergoosepublishing.com

Who Will Love the Crow

COPYRIGHT © 2016 by Miriam Dunn

First Edition, May 2016

Cover Design by Winter Goose Publishing
Typesetting by Odyssey Books
Photography by Olivia Ellen MacDonald

ISBN: 978-1-941058-48-0

Published in the United States of America

Contents

Deconstruction of the Poet	1
Fly Aways	2
Each Moment Sweet	3
Quiet-tide	5
Kenzieville Curve	6
Blue	8
Spiral	9
Tears in Oceans	10
The Clock	11
Who Will Love the Crow?	14
Albescence	15
Pilgrims	17
Discovery	18
Shadow	19
Autumn's Descent	21
Young Winds	23
Paths	24
Earth Trembles	25
Fall Again	28
Legs	29
Angels	32
I Dreamed a Shore	33
Whistles Trickling	34
A Word	36
Hunger	37
This, My Heart	40
Guards	42

These Soft Words	44
Geisha	45
From My Mouth	46
To See for You	48
Old Words	50
Collecting Confessions	52
Soft	54
The Dream	55
The Next Word	56
Harvesting the Fog	58
Midnight	60
Undressed	61
Gifts	63
The Ocean Is Too Big	64
Dead	66
Metaphor is Meat	68
Crows	69
The Hush	71
Ele Disse	73
The Painting	74
No Poetry	75
sTAgES	77
Night Time Walkers	78
Almost	79
The Beginning	80
In the Winter Frost	82
Innocent & the Sage	84
Boy	85
Not Silence	87

Seasons	89
Your Fire	90
Marble	92
Sacred	93
Waves	94
Crescent Moon	95
Burnings and Breathings	96
The Space	97
Half Spooned	98
The Whole of It	101
These Two Open Hands	102
Holy	103
Edge of Beauty	105
A Place	106
somewhen between	108
Still, Dover Beach	109
Trees Weeping	111
This, That, and Another Thing	112
Red	114
Captive on a Ship	115
Acknowledgments	117
About the Author	119

To my mom and dad, of course

Deconstruction of the Poet

I tell you my secrets
on the white of winter
in first snow;
whispers so warm
they melt paths of confessions
leaving trails of trampled notions
and blood-red ideas.

A voice freezes before it forms a single truth
in the hoary glass.
Reflections are dead
in this cold season of sadness.

Follow

Arctic syllables
fall
from
the
sky,
touch down, one after another;

their meaning buried beneath
a drift of words;

pretense ploughed
and piled too high to climb.

The cold sound of a pen scratch.

Fly Aways

In between the random and intent
between chaos and the must-be-dones
waves and lines of openness
and closed
the fly-aways and foxtrot
we walk

hearts open
behind the gate
eyes deep
before the look-aways
lips parted
to speak

do not love me
do
love me
not
do
love

Each Moment Sweet

The silver haze of days
have moved too fast,
rushing like a stream out to a sea.
Starless skies that rise and fall
like rivers crawl
toward the night, then fall
inside of me.

The late days of our journey
are turning cold;
the monuments we built to love, decay.
All but the sun and moon and stars
are getting old;
night's ebony turns into silver grey.

Though every time of joy,
each moment sweet,
have long since lost their blossoms, dead and gone,
buried, ever there, the seeds at our feet,
the bouquet of our memories,
the love we've known.

In spite of swiftly-moving years,
one thing stays true:
All the love you've ever loved,
remains with you.

Quiet-tide

river reflection
quiet-tide of harvest night
grandmother Moon wakes

Kenzieville Curve

When you pass through Kenzieville Curve
Earth hugs you.

You are in a mother valley,
cradled.

One turn leads to another
and before you know it
you have been waltzed.

In autumn,
you are enveloped in a dappled curtain of colour.

In winter,
steep sides of warm white
stand sentinel.

At night,
you enter the womb
and are reborn.

When you pass through Kenzieville Curve
something happens soul deep.

It is like
cool air that travels on the coat tails of a still, sizzling summer breeze,
an impossible existence,
yet it flutters across your face, nonetheless.

It is like
a melody that marches along
obedient to the lead line
then bursts into a Halleluiah harmony,
scoops you up
into an impossible seventh note,
then sets you down,
breathless.

It is like
finding a battered top hat on the side of a country road,
or blue bird sea glass on a mountain side,
or an old wicker chair set on an impossible pristine plain of
snow-covered winter wheat.

A cold dive in icy water
that turns warm.

When you pass through Kenzieville Curve
Earth hugs you,
and you are coming home.

Blue

Woke up from the flannel of my dreams
and everything was blue
yet the velvet crush of sleep against my skin
had promised something new

the night was swollen
wet with wish
and rained the desert dry
sun loosed my footing from the earth
and turned me to the sky

Spiral

      do you feel it?
descending down beauty
        obsidian clear

cascade
      tumbling
                         sea spiral
              echoes

into
pin point nothing

darkness
as empty as forget
as wide as unimagined

Tears in Oceans

I found our secrets
like stones tossed on a pebbled beach
a tiny grain
on a sandy strand
or words lost
and out of reach

tears in oceans
our breath in air
hanging still
and stiller, still,
than all the wind that is not there

I found our secrets
black in night
and white on light
a hunter hunched behind a blind
horizon when it's out of sight
sunrise
when the day's behind

I found our secrets
salt in the sea
the hot in heat
the you in me

The Clock
For Granny McGee

I have a clock next to by my bed.
Every night
it keeps me awake.

unceasing stilettos on slate

It reminds me of you

and my last trip
to the top
of
those
narrow
stairs

to your room,
warm enough to hatch chicks.

You wanted water
or maybe another blanket
or maybe just to know what time it was
because I looked at that clock,
and I hated it.

taunting tapping on tiny legs

No need to say,
no clock was ever so melancholy
or so succinctly reminded one
of the meticulous, measured, march of the minutes,
the hours,
the days,
the months.

Louder than any clock need be,
it haunted my creaking climb to you.

punctuating pain with perfect precision

And there you lay,
unmoving,
a crepe-paper doll,
cold,
cocooned within the quiet of quilts.

I could never understand why you kept that clock,
how in that cloistered room time could have any meaning.

The silence between the seconds was life
      holding its breath,
the narrative of a house dying.

It had been a home
that made up the mystery of my mother's life.
And now it was an old house
with a clock
and a death
that took more time than ever need be.

I was twelve years old
yet at the top of the stair I wished I were younger
and could creep, courageous and silent,
into your camphor rooms as I once did,
and slide my fingers across
the forbidden bric-a-brac of your life.

the secrecy of knick-knacks and dust

I was afraid
that if I lingered a little longer
the clock would stop.

I wanted to tell you I loved you
but time ran out.

Who Will Love the Crow?

everyone loves the Raven
but who will love the crow?

dropping
secrets
into
the
deep
of
night
from
her
eternal
sky

too dark
are midnight words
lost
behind the moon
carried by a trickster

Albescence

Thoughts of you,
albescence,
white drifting, drifting.

Once alit,
wind-blown soft
and lifting, lifting.

Through the ice-bone fingers fall,
sifting, sifting.

Running river point of time
is shifting, shifting.

Pilgrims

day's sleepy saunter
—we are horizon pilgrims
end to end dreaming

Discovery

Scarcely being black
attention was made
one to another
recognized eagerly
nodding
knowing
each pointed out their own dark eyes
fixed lips begged for wishes
possession of curiosity
terminated
in discovery of each other

Shadow

Shadow had spent his life in a prison
in the darkest dark he'd ever know.
Every time Old Sol had risen
he'd stretch across
the world below.

And all that time he cursed the sun
not knowing that the two were one

Shadow had lived in solitaire
once the birds had left the sky.
Every night with Darkness there
he'd watch for Moon
in her saunter by.

He'd watch the Moon in her nightly race
not knowing how he kissed her face

Shadow had done
what shadows will do
trapped in a freedom, free in his cell.
Without the Shadow
where is Light?
Where is the Beauty,
and how could we tell?

He kissed the ground as Sun passed by
not knowing he held up the sky

Autumn's Descent

Autumn's descent
drifts

not lightly

but as a shadowed shawl
of heavy

the decay of days
ablaze
beneath a brooding sky

last leaves protest
the dowsing of their final fire
but like the early eves
must fall

Young Winds

breathe us to the new
old givings are not wasted
tethered to young winds

Paths

Even the wind has left
the ghost towns of Utopia,
where rattled chains
of lovers lost
haunt the still blue air.
But ancient loves,
once found again,
stay on the labyrinth path
that leads again
to empty arms
that still await them there.

Earth Trembles

I am Earth.
And, Traveler
I can feel you.

I feel you in the twilight.

I feel your steps coming to me,
treading to the sound of my heart pounding.

I feel your hands,
dark fingers exploring milky crevices,

your open palms pressing
on the cool and moist,

face against face,
climbing higher,

your body strong against me,
crossing mountains.

I feel your thirsty mouth
drinking from me
and I give more to quench you.

I feel your breath,
hot,
moving swiftly over restless seas,
touching me like moonlight on waves.

Your breath,

hungry and humming,
heavy and hushed,
stirring dust in still deserts.

Fields sway like music when you exhale,
trees bend low at your impatience,

waters swell.

You open your arms
and the sun rises in them,
the moon moves the tides in my hips,

ebony shroud blankets white flesh,
frost melts away
sweet dew,
slippery lips on lips.

Earth trembles.

Mountains crumble beneath your gaze,
beneath your fingertips.

Seas rush in to me
and leave in the sweet rhythm
of our selves.

Gaia quakes
exposing secret places,
dangerous and beautiful.

Traveler, I am Earth.
And I still feel you.

Fall Again

What if I
should confess
to something less
than that which goes unnamed?
Would my sentence be the same
or all forgiven
and none to blame
for falling from the place
where I just fell?

Would all be well
knowing that
the landing
is no harder than
this standing
still
without a will
to fall again?

Legs

doctors have a way
(of handing over news like this)
his eyes
skewer me

breach my skull and pin me to the air

yet
somehow
the
floor
seems
closer

doctors have a way
(of lending you their steady gaze)
as
they
grocery
list
the
way
the
world
just
ended

Eyes pinned,
I stay afloat in a sea of difference,
and treading there I dare to watch his lips move.

every
thing
I
know
no
longer
matters

and I am several inches
closer to the floor

severed

having legs
makes no sense now
pinned to the air
like this

Angels

they will look like me
if god would send her angels
they will look like you

I Dreamed a Shore

I dreamed a shore
where the waves did not go out,
the waves did not come in.

Crests frozen white,
sand beneath captured in chaos,
not asking to be swept up,
not asking to be brought home,
or brought anywhere.

Eternal and hidden,
never having known the difference
between the surface and the deep,
the surface and the darkness,
dancing in the infinite tide
that has ceased.

Hidden.

Pressed upon by the will of the moon,
released in a havoc not understood.

And the waves return to where they were first conceived,
to when I believed
the tide would rock me gently
and keep the promise of that first rhythm.

Coming to me . . . *leaving from me* . . .

Coming to me.

Whistles Trickling

Whistles trickling
Can that be so?

Trickling Hopscotch
Stubbing Noises
Tripping Pavement
Squeals a-flutter
Tossing Rhythms
Bloody Promise
Small Stone Treasure
Doorstep Dreaming
Ancient Voices
Escaping Barefoot
Spinning Monsters
Long Grass Kissing
Riding Hilltops
Apples Smoking
Waking Freckles
Sun Consuming
Swinging Clutches
Pocket Secrets
Bulrush Scepter
Shadows Changing
Whistles Trickling
Trickling Hopscotch
Hopscotch Dreaming
Can that be so?

A Word

What if I disturb you
with a word
that once lay hid
within a shell
then flew off like a bird;
its careless beak
dropping
sounds
that once have met the air
reassembled nonsense syllables
and were reconstructed there?

What if I should move you
with a thought
once buried deep within a grave
that Earth, herself, forgot
its restless sleep
that once aroused,
began to breach the ground
and sang a dirge to happiness
while making not a sound?

Hunger

We spent hours on the hillside,
noses inches away from blades of grass,
looking for four-leaf clovers
with our perfect eyes.
Surely if there were some anywhere,
they would be here.

Then we rolled
arms
crossed
over chests
we rolled
down
the steep
bodies tumbling
over
and again
plummeting
to the bottom
and slowed into laughter

The earth spun past in shrieks.

Hunger.
No need to go home.
We looked for sweet-sally saucers.
They would be tasty and filling enough.
Who could eat more?

We could eat grass, if it came to that.
And tiny strawberries the size of pin heads.
Or we could rub some sap from the tree,
chew it
and call it gum.
Who could chew the longest?

We knew where rhubarb and blackberries grew wild.
There was a garden to raid, if it came to that.
We took long stalks of grass with fuzzy heads and chewed
them until our hunger went
and you said I looked like Tom Sawyer.

We spread love across the world in dandelions.

When the clouds moved in
we lay on our backs,
arms behind our heads,
and searched for faces of the dead.
You saw your mother.
I looked for God but found nothing.

This, My Heart

This, my heart,
my country,
terrain folded and bent,
uprising in swells,
mountains leveled,
rivers cut through wildness like swords,

seeds blown,

arrows sent into the mist
against an enemy unseen.

This, my heart, my country,
beneath which dream lost souls
blooming hyacinth and lilies.

Wind still carries voices of the lost
songs of the fallen
and me.

A wind eternal,
infinite lament,
a lullabyadirgearequiem.

This, my heart
that has been scorched,
terrain that has been home and hell.

Above the putrid black
still soars one bird
with allegiance only to the sky.

Above, beneath,
lips on lips,

metal on metal,

metal to bone,

one blood mingled in a restless pool.

And I still walk the hills
aghostawarrioraprisoner,

a ruler without borders of a nameless land that is my heart.

Guards

The keeper of faith
guards the gate
though every soldier surrender;
my heart is a winter,
frozen and still,
forgotten by those who defend her.

In a frozen drift
on a land with no ruler
legions still march, white on white;
the ghosts of my dreams
wander the path
of my heart,
that is darker than night.

WWII 36th Field Battery in Sydney Mines, Cape Breton

These Soft Words

These soft words
shall gentle our condition
and our condition, gentled,
shall be our daily balm.
Echoes of our whispers
into the abyss fall;
storms tumble through the chasm,
soothed sweetly into calm.

Forgetful of calamity
beneath the river runs,
swept by the careless current of our dreams;
above the rippling tide of days
hope cradles us along
in oceans born
of our two crossing streams.

Geisha

The ghost of the Geisha
moves in still winds;
in her whiteness the dance disappears.
Bones have been crushed
and powdered to dust
and settle like snow on the years.

From My Mouth

At night
we trade secrets
that morning will burn
in a fire of regret
leaving tongues scorched

Je te serre dans mes bras

There are no words
just ashes left
that move on the winds of darkness
from where we meet
and settle in faraway day places
where we are alone

el corazon de mi corazon

Always, I come to you filled
and leave speechless

you empty the words
from my mouth
and fill me with longing

reste toujours avec moi

To See for You

Today I use my eyes to see for you

Catch the sun
falling
                on the sea

      Waves billow
breathing diamonds
       back into the lungs of wind

Gull hovers and dives
               departs upon a current
                          circles on his
                    own mysterious path
and in his majestic white returns, untired, back to me

Ripples reach the shore
       between ocean breaths

Horizon spread like a line-fresh sheet
just crumpled by love's morning

Something drifts
               and peeks and hides
            behind the coming waves that
           rock me in familiar ways
             a small white
              coming and going

        And I sit here
on my ocean of rock
        stone waves trapped upon the shore

   still

Old Words

I found these old words,
well used.
The tide of days brought them to me
polished
and made me think of lilacs
and canyons
and a matchbox home
with a claw-foot tub big enough for two.

They made me think of letters
addressed to Darling,
signed with love,

and days when I believed
I held your heart in my hand
like a stone.

Collecting Confessions

She travelled at night
collecting confessions,
tossed your regrets
in an apron of sky,
shook all the blossoms
from trees not yet blooming,
fed them to birds
who could no longer fly,

polished your dreams
she found on the sea shore,
offered them back
to an ocean of days,
ignited the light
that was caverned in darkness,
ended beginnings in mysterious ways.

She tore down the alter
built with your wishes,
let go the slaves
who carried your dreams,
folded the day
you spread like a blanket,
smoothed 'cross the morning
that ripped at night's seams,

smiled at your demons
who stared from the deepness
of still standing water
drowning your praise,
severed the kite strings
tied to your mourning
then swallowed the blood
and slid 'cross the blade,

ignited the light
that was caverned in darkness,
ended beginnings
in mysterious ways.

Soft

the unbearable posture
of impermanence

bowed
hoping and bowed
knowing and bowed
finger-tipping the last light
before the sky blankets us

humbled at love's feet
too large to be
too small to be
just being

like the smooth of a pear's skin
beneath the edge of sharpness

becoming naked

and soft

The Dream

When the dream's upon us
beneath our patch of sky
and all about us moves
except the dreamer,
hopes attach themselves to stars
and slowly saunter by;
only daylight shall be our redeemer.

In the shadows darkly
below the curve of dawn
diffused and brilliant,
rising into view,
are wishes cast upon the sun
that, gentle, light the way
and carry your intentions back to you.

The Next Word

Waiting for the next word:

unchained
clandestine
clever calamitousness
serendipitous seriousity
plain perspectivity
brave, bold nonsense
anchored
alit
aloft

Love in a lantern?
Pockets of regret?

A kaleidoscope of questions careening to corners.

Rolling clouds of angry adjectives bursting open with wet meaning.

A runaway train of unruly nouns unpackaged, undelivered.

The next word.

Promises make pinholes in our hearts.

Water is my favorite,
the darling of all metaphors:

sweetly sweeping
clearly cleansing
too wild, too deep
polishing perfect pebbles
drowning a dead man's dreams
watery graves of good intentions

Rocks, too.

ancient and ever
thoughts too heavy
lives that skip along the surface
and end up dry on dresser bureaus
or filling pockets
or looming like Wordworth's mountain

marble memory
winter windows
clocks and compass
blood and thistle

Waiting, still, to tumble down.

Harvesting the Fog

Untangling the silence,
harvesting the fog,
the sky is such a perfect place for sleep;
a gallery of forgotten things
in a castle built from laughter;
the visitors lock lovers in the keep.

They come to see the future gone
some time before the Fall,
before the Dream Collector earns his pay;
but all they see are mirrors broken on the wall
and empty eyes stare back from yesterday.

The music that the ocean plays,
some say it is a dirge,
others say the tide's own lullaby;
the symphony of never-was is a single note that's heard
by all the dreamers sleeping in my sky.

Untangling the silence, harvesting the fog,
the wing-ed things can't rest above a sea;
this world's no place for dreamers
flying all alone,
and now I know
the sky's too big for me.

Midnight

ocean of midnight
wading in warm wakefulness
riverbed of dreams

Undressed

Your Sun rises
over this Horizon

the cupped curve of my hips
the smooth line of my back
arched

and sets again
in the valley
between these mountains
covered in the softness of my skin

Your Breath
the breeze that taunts my flesh

Your Tongue
the morning moist
that awakens the sleeping garden

Your Body
the Celestial Star
that twins my own
ever orbiting in the Universe of my Love

And
I
am
undressed

by
your
eyes

forever moving
from day to night
beneath
the hunger
of your gaze.

Gifts

In broken wishbones
and night's first star,

in the peacefulness
of the sleeping baby's breath,

are my discoveries of Mother's Love.

Hopeful.
Healing.
Potent and Sublime.

Sifting through these Glory Gifts,
I emerge
triumphant and whole,
a single note
spirited from the Angel's Trumpet.

The Ocean Is Too Big

I see your face above the surface
in the sun's frenzied rain
that dances on this sea.

Moving toward me?

And beyond, a sailboat, like a ghost
forever sailing,
longing for a shore.
Like us.

The ocean is too big
but still I feel you.

The ocean is too big
and yet I dare to cross each night
hopeful and exhausted,
drenched in longing
strengthened and weakened all at once.

I will paint this.

Dip my brush in mercury.
Dip my brush in mist,
some marmalade,
some rays of night and sun and summer rain.

Dip my brush in all the words
that are yet formed.

Dip my brush in longing,
then dip again.

Dead

Do you remember the quicksand
and its gurgling swallow
of all that is alive?
Deadly smother,
a gurgling swallow of all last words
that ever were.

Well, I have found them,

those sandy mud-filled choking words
that are buried.

Reaching down into the muck of life,
palms up, accepting blessings from the muses
dry, dirt dead.

Quicksand deep lost feeling.

Love

gurgling,
choked,

rising up,
delivering this,
my poem,
to
you.

Metaphor is Meat

chew to the bone
of this once poem
metaphor is meat

suck
the fat of allusion
there's never enough to eat

start salting the stanza
pepper the prose
dice up the rhythm
of syllabic feet
go down on the grizzle
lick up the spice
tongue the tercet
savour the sweet

metaphor is meat

Crows

Here
you can see the cold;
the ghosts of winter reveal themselves
and whiten our words
as they leave our mouths.

We talk about the crows,

smart birds, they say.

There was an experiment once.

I saw one open a lunch box and take out the cookies, stacked them just so—

Until someone interrupts to correct us.

Ravens, he says, *not crows.*

Bigger than crows.

Yes. And smarter, too.

Saw one last week stack crackers in a pile before carrying them off.

Smart, they are.

And all the while
the frost spirits
hang in the air around us,

we stomp our feet
and take a last puff of a cigarette
under watchful eyes.

The Hush

This is the hush of earth as she's spinning;
here's the lament of yesterday gone.
This is the quiet of memories leaving,
the death rattle rhythm that sings like a song.

Here is the daylight feasting on darkness;
this is horizon swallowed by night.
Here is the dance of the days and the minutes,
the rush of their wings as they take to flight.

Here is the ocean moving like quicksand;
this is the moon that worships the tide.
Here are the waves that run from the shoreline,
burying dreams we all cast aside.

Here is the groan of the mountain that rises;
this is the whimper of plans laid to die.
Here is the fall of today and tomorrow,
drops in the river of time passing by.

Niagara Falls, Canadian side

Ele Disse

Disse
Não me duvides. És bonita.
E eu usei seus olhos como espelhos e me transformei.
Disse
Eu sou maior do que o oceano
e eu confiei que o mundo era pequeno
e coloquei-o em minhas mãos.
Disse
Vem até mim
E pouco a pouco conduziu-me, iluminando o trajeto com esperança,
Retornando-me para casa com amor.
Disse
Dê-me todos os seus dias maus.
E eu assim fiz.
Um por um, eu dei-lhe, até ele ficar cheio.
Disse
Eu sinto-te.
E eu quebrei-me num caleidescópio de cor
e disse, sentes-me agora?
Disse.
E mais não disse.

The Painting

There was no freedom
in the frame
except the upturned urn
its flowers spilled—
a river of magenta
daring to flow beyond the edges
past its wooden prison.

We imagined lanterns hanging overhead,
the source of the cadmium stream that rivered yellow from
unseen rafters
casting shadows on the cobalt

Surely there was life
elsewhere beyond the still.

Perhaps off in the distance,
or very near,
beyond the umber and crimson,
people stirred
and talked and loved
and made music that could not be heard.

No Poetry

There is no poetry
in these words
. . . no birds

no candlelight
or long forbidden walks
or talks

no wind that blows
or seed that grows
no angel wings
no angel things
at all

no metaphor
about a shore
and how you are the tide
that rushes up to greet me
no rocks
no polished pebbles
uncut stones
no bleeding hearts or buried bones

no desert quenched
no love's lament

no symphony in river's song
no quiet place where we belong
no drum that only we can hear
no nothings sweetly in my ear
no rhythm pulsing through our veins
no poetry
so what remains
are pages white
no ink is spilled
silent night
no hearts are filled

No poetry are in these words

sTAgES

The stages of his sadness
are understood
by those who know the rhythm of regret,
the accidental sharps and flats of notes
that do not fit,
the sweet and soulful slip into minor chords that once were
major,
the exquisite sorrow of one diminished.

He began in thirds
and by the time he drank his sixth,
his heart played a seventh,
then a ninth,
and by the time he lit a second smoke while one still burned
in the ashtray;
by the time he started calling old lovers;
by the time he was singing to old ballads
and crying along to the last waltz played at his high school
prom,
everything was augmented,

and more,
and there,
and real,

and so brilliantly clear he knew he could sleep
and start again tomorrow.

Night Time Walkers

And there you are
pulling me
as I play like one helpless
because I love the pull
and I love that you are there
even when you are not
even when you are dark and hiding
even when
you tip your gaze and
shadow all our longing
in the cradle of your form

you follow me
I follow you
to the dark side
to the other side
and our mysteries
hide like night time walkers

and there you are

Almost

it was almost like night
the long shadow of day
stretched taut across our knowing
the sharp habit of breathing and beating and being
ground down by the edges of forgetfulness

it was almost like night
metal moments etched in tarnishings
one whole life
carried around in a head full of dull and dreaming
a sepia trudge through fallen things

The Beginning

There is
the beginning,
the cascade from nothing into all that was.
A nothing,
yet it flowed
and
tumbled,

alit
gently,
unexpected, like the blackbird

escaped from dark,
escaped from stability,
reckless.

Poured out and shouted out
from the singularity of selflessness,

freedom,

the inexplicable
un-pronounceable
dare-not sayable
glossolalia of
freedom.

Everything but skin is shed,
surely this is leverage with the gods.

Freedom
because no soul dare stagnate in sanguine opposition to a moving sky,

endless sky,

beginning and endless,

intense nothing
there
in the beginning.

In the Winter Frost

They left their baby in the winter frost.
They will walk into his room tonight,
look at his bed, empty,
his small pillow,
baseball blankets and plastic dinosaurs,
and
they
will
fall

to

their

knees,

blind into each other's arms,

into unthinkable, unspeakable, furious emptiness.

Furious emptiness,
furious defeat,
furious love that is sent out like rockets and land nowhere,
furious silence that implodes with the hungry noise of sorrow,
furious freezing of the heart.

It makes one weak to even think of them.

You must lie prone at the bottom of their hearts
and witness those hearts shatter and fall in flames down upon you,
grotesque and dangerous.

Furious.

Furious and full,
furious and empty,
furious with gentle love.
Grotesque and dangerous in each other's arms.

They left their baby in the winter's frost.

Innocent & the Sage

Pushing the sun over horizon
Innocent mourned
the darkness behind

Always her eyes
were lifted above her
into the light
that rendered her blind

Holding the sun
in the center of skyward
the arms of the Sage
were weary and old

One step ahead
of the day as it travelled
dragging her thoughts
from the heat to the cold

One saw the light
that lured her on upwards
One kept on moving
the light trailed behind

Together the spectrum
of days were their lovers
as they dreamed of longing
they both designed

Boy

I crept down stealth,
        pathways jagged he left open
into secret places.

Boy hiding.

When I woke him,
ready to be in my arms.
When I touched him,
ready to run.

When the dark and quiet hid him in love's openness
I pretended not to know his name,
pretended not to know:
two score years is a long time to be alone,
ungrown.

Pathways jagged we have traveled; entered whole and left
fragmented.

My empty spaces,
voluminous,
fill him.

fissures filled with hurt like putty gushing

He blocks entry with my bareness;
takes my nothing and turns it into mortar and brick.

Yet something seeps.
And now he's left the scent of his long sleep on me.
And what am I to do with that?

Not Silence

You will think I have no strength left,
barely breathing.
Eyes dust-clouded, kicked up from years lived.
I may want darkness, but not silence.
As I drift toward the river
the greedy boatman picking bones from rotting teeth
waits with grim impatience for my patronage.
I shall fire up my will,
fan that pyre with the heat of my recent youth.
I will curse
and ask for one last drink.

Let's wrestle in the sounds and smells of my life gone by.
Not in silence.
Bring me music,
haunting, shocking, pointless, poignant.
I shall like to drift away lost in something raucous and
complex.

Fan the aroma of fresh baked bread, clothesline linen,
and apple pies until the cinnamon and yeast, vibrant and
powerful, waft throughout my dying chamber.
Deny the stench of my decaying cells and slothful blood.
Not silence.
Laughter.
Laughter and children—squealing, teasing, crying.
Let them come with dirty faces and ill manners and
questions uncomfortable for mothers to hear.

Not silence.
Your voice.
Loud and irreverent.
Dance.
Be an accomplice to my death.
Make it noisy.
and I shall do my part.

Seasons

Four faces of meaning
The seasons' intent
The change in the stillness
The winter's lament
The fruit of spring's labors
In summer's ferment
The deep into darkness
Of autumn's decent
Days march like words
That we never meant
As we mark on the clock
The time we misspent

Your Fire

You think there is no fire,
you and I in this winter built for two.
When you reach out your hands
cold crystals kiss your fingertips.

Here is your fire.
Here is your heat.
Here is your macabre romance
footstepping the disconnected movements of our day,
burning.

Our love was born hot into the frost that cradles us like snow blankets,
forged into scorching ice solitude.

Our love,
melting
in messy forgetfulness,
streaming only slight discomfort
rivers away from us.

This is our cool ocean of dying
and we, in it,
are motionless and warm in its liquid melancholy.

From our submerged place we reach up to the frozen surface
(the crystal clarity of the cascade constant above us),
shattered by the polarity of ourselves,
drowning in the ice-covered liquid abandonment of
ourselves.

But we have no choice.
We reach
into the cold crystals that kiss our fingertips.
That is you.
That is me.
That is.
This is your fire,
the warm departure melting every hoary heartbreak.

Marble

I rise to the frost on the window
and become the landscape beyond,
blanketed with white in the darkness
dying.

My feet touch cold floors
and I become marble,
stilled.
Safe,
not falling,
not flying.

Sacred

tomorrow's shadow
stretched through sacred yesterdays
light of earth's longing

Waves

I wait for the big ones,
stand defiant and pressed against.
I wait to see if they'll wash anything away,
take some damage from me,
cleanse the shame that covers my skin like black oil on
feathers,
carry it out to sea
or to the shore
or simply let it sink
or rise.

But I will not submerge my eyes.
It is strength enough to stand and let the ocean rock me.
The soft beneath may fall away and swallow me;
the blue above may drop and cover me.
I will not submerge.

It is the motion, perhaps,
because it moves me,
pushes me,
tests my strength against it,
allows me to believe, briefly, that I can withstand anything.

There is something behind my eyes
and it wants to go home
to the sea.

Crescent Moon

A crescent moon hangs low from the winter sky,
a sad sideways slumber of white lighting the frosty glass of
night's open window.
The cold breeze battles against the screen, touching my flesh
like feather fingertips;
a smooth scribe on my shoulders.

I am laid out bare beneath the eyes of night imagining you
are the wind,
rushing over my open field.

But when the heat of you leaves me
I am, again,
curled against my emptiness
alone
beneath a crescent moon.

Burnings and Breathings

There are secrets in the desert.
Ancient forgivings.
Buried losings and longings.

Sun knows herself there and
smiles when night-time's sisters shine.

Dark turns in and out again
Tireless watchings
Fallings and risings
Ancient touchings
Forsaken fires

Lives not ripened
Short endings buried

Burnings and breathings
Scuttling dances
Foot prints gone

Old sands drift over
Knowings and lettings
Opals in snake eyes
Heat hiding hot liftings

Old sands drift over
Lovings and namings
Wild jewels and drum beatings
Share desert secrets

The Space

This cannot be taught
and this cannot be known:
the deep stillness of our being,
the glass before it's blown;

the spokes within the wheel,
the empty pot, the seed unsown;
the block of wood
that's not been carved;
the jeweled, but empty, throne;

the pinpoint of existence,
before the fire was spread
in ashes of our longing;
the word, before it's said,

the continent that was our heart
before the ocean grew
and moved us close together
in the space between the two.

Half Spooned

Pushed away
my good-sleep nights

Guardian
at the Gate of Dreams

Holder of the wide-awakes

Holder of me

Uncurled
Unfurled

Half-spooned
Draft-spooned
Cold at my back

Wrapped in his nothing
Cloaked in his gone-away

Now they crawl in bold
between awakes and asleeps and heat

dropping
danger
and
dead things

I do not trust the night
that leaves rendered sheets unholy
and dreams not fit for dreamers
like me

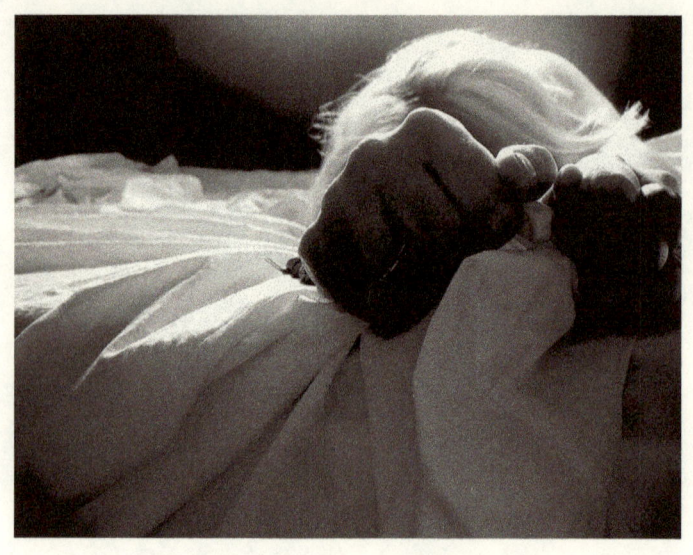

The Whole of It

Have you seen the wind teasing leaves on the pavement?
frenzied tackling

Right there. That's life.
The whole of it.

The color of fire going out,
dried and fallen . . .
Swept up nuisance taken by surprise,
stirred,
battled,
clinging,

fighting lightly.

Beauty and waste.
Time and forgotten.
Overpowered whirlwind of decay.

Life.
Right there.

The whole of it.

These Two Open Hands

In these two open hands
I hold your beating heart—
and swallow all the tears that you have cried.
Arms cradle you in comfort,
slow rock you like the waves
and hold you like the ocean holds the tide.

I will gather all your worries
like leaves upon the breeze
and carry them to places not yet known—
And all that will be left for you
is Love and Heart and Me,
for everything but Us shall be wind-blown.

Holy

You wear a crown of sins
bowed at the altar of your pain.
You're here to serve the multitudes
the poison of your reign;
with your mouth full of wisdom
and eyes sewn shut by fear,
your genuflecting image
is sold as a souvenir.

The candles dance your shadows
but your body never moves
to the symphony of madness,
but all your mirrors prove
there is a blind man that is watching
as the fires burn around;
the altar of your righteousness
crumbles to the ground.

You spend your nights
with pilgrims,
barefoot and walking slow,
holding hands with sinners
who never asked to go
on the mission of your madness
as your drummers keep the beat;
waiting for the silence
so you can wash their bloody feet.

Your gospel has been written
by the voices in your head.
You whip the backs of lovers
and praise the living dead
who bury all their laughter
in a tomb behind a stone
and pocket their forgiveness
as they kneel before your throne.

Where the soulless wander,
you cannot say for sure;
but the dead shall do the living
in honour of your war.
The bones are climbed like mountains
and once the battle's won
the final thing of beauty
will hang like the morning sun.

Edge of Beauty

On the mountain edge of beauty,
beneath a sky of dreams,
wishes are like raindrops
that waterfall and stream,
descending on a path
to your ocean, wide with time;
your footing starts to shift
like a dreamer's paradigm.

You know the edge is wasting;
you know the sky may fall.
You know the path you follow
leads to nowhere new, at all.
And time is still a-wasting
with much nothing left to do,
but you spread your arms to fly—
for the dreamer still in you.

A Place

I have a place with dark secret pathways
the hours pass by for my own amusement
hollow back-stairways
uninviting and weaving
with hardly a light
to show shadows leaving
stepways on steroids
beneath my feet heaving
threatening to speak of my comings and goings.

I have a place with wild secret nonsense
I chatter in rhyme and fumble my words
whisper and writhe and foretell of one coming
with hooves and umbrellas
and sex in a bottle
incantations and whistles
my fingertips drumming.

I have a place with dread secret passages
I juggle your dreams if you dare to listen
to my travels and playtime
my wailing and rapping
my haunting and laughter
mad meaningless singing
I creep along
never boring of darkness
but conjure up company
for no special reason.

somewhen between

somewhen between the veil and the day
the color of singing
the cool sound of blue

somewhere I lean against breath of the sky
and touch the horizon
that curls into you

sometime I gather the scent of my dreaming
and fold up the night
in pockets of sand
then sweep up the notions that rain from the darkness
tumbling like fire
to the palm of my hand

Still, Dover Beach

The ebb and flow of love,
smooth pebbles tossed against the shore,
leaves unbelievers lost,
rough tumbled in its roar.

Pale specter of the world,
its shadows fall on darkling plain;
white cliffs will still loom tall
'ere crumbling once again.

And melancholy night
in timeless paths across the sky,
are stilled by lovers' words,
though long centuries pass them by.

For rivers of our time
still interweave with currents past;
covenants conceived,
collected like sea-glass.

A note hangs in the air:
the channel's cry at end of day,
voluminous with life,
before its sweet decay.

And there still hangs the moon,
on Dover's tide, its plaintive song;
eternal notes abide.
Sea of faith still moves as strong.

Old Sophocles could hear
the voice of time within the spray;
and now the voice is mine,
lest my words be washed away.

The ebb and flow of time,
a love sea-tossed against the strand,
retreat and then return,
back to the moon-blanched land.

Trees Weeping

Dreamed of phantom thoughts and rocks
A perfume pallet of broken clocks
Smokey desert's sun ablaze
With midnight birds lost in the days
And I could not tell light from down
Gem mountains floating all around
Trees weeping for their lost starfish
On falling waves, I made my wish
That rubies would all still be blue
And I could sing like opals do
The sapphire sky would drop its net
And capture all that I'd forget.

This, That, and Another Thing

Zig and Zag were such a drag;
she would sing & he would nag.
And no matter what Zig did,
Zag would always flip his lid.
And no matter where Zag went
Zig showed up so she could vent.
They trudged through life, through highs and lows;
Zig and Zag—strange bed-fellows.
Stranger still, you must agree,
is the story of their family.
Zig would dance upon a grave!
Zag would never be so brave.
Zig danced upon a table top!
Zag begged and prayed that she would stop.
Yes Zig and Zag were quite the drag;
she loved to speed but he would lag.
So Zig and Zag just led their life—
he going left, her faking right.
Never were there worse a match
than Mr. This and Mrs. That.
This and That could not agree;
she'd order wine—he'd bring her tea.
And This, so dull, could take no more
of That entering through the exit door.
And taking off the mattress tag!
Life on the edge was not his bag.
Zag digged This and that was that.

Poor Zig was stunned but there she sat,
till she was face to face with That
thinking "This" was tit for tat!

Zag fell for This and made his pledge.
Zig and That live on the edge.
That loved Zig so gave a ring . . .
But then walked in Another Thing!

Soon came babies Hum and Haw.
Everyone looked but No One saw
that Hum looked like Zig
but Haw looked like That,
Hum was thin but Haw was fat.

Someone exclaimed, "Something's odd,"
and with a wink and then a nod,
No One said "Yes, I agree."
No One could sort this family tree.
How could Hum belong to That
and how could Haw have been begat
by This and Zag? The little brat!

Life will go on, for Zag and This,
That and Zig, they will not miss,
but Hum and Haw will always be
torn between their family.

Red

If this were a poem,
which it is not,
it would fall red droplets
and stain.

If this were a song,
I would sing it to you
once
then never again.

If this were a painting,
I'd paint it with blue
then wash it away
with the rain.

If this were my heart,
I would break it in two
and nothing of me
would remain.

Captive on a Ship

Captive on a vessel
that sails us back to where we are,
amid a sea of darkness
the birthing of a star
wandering time through smooth and storm,
too close to suns that never warm
against the rocks
we're tossed, alone.
Freedom is a journey.

Freedom is a journey
that ends where it begins,
cast off the ropes that bind you,
set your sail against the winds,
navigate between the isles,
there is not rest for miles and miles,
captive on a ship.

Freedom's only for the brave
who sail above a watery grave,
captive on a ship.

Acknowledgments

Poetry writing, for me, was a solitary exercise for many years. Scattered throughout my living space, often scribbled illegibly on loose papers and countless notebooks strewn on shelves and in boxes, only on rare occasions did my compositions reach the eyes of others. Social media changed all that as I began to share my work, often receiving warm and supportive feedback from people across the globe.

I have made many friends over the years through these wonderful platforms that permit us to reveal many aspects of ourselves and feel I must acknowledge the huge role that my online connections have played in encouraging me. These many and varied associations, which I value deeply, have fostered a belief in myself and my work which I think would otherwise have been unattainable. Thank you to my irreplaceable online community of friends who continue to cheer me on, sharing in the excitement of the release of my first collection.

I would like to acknowledge fellow poet, Frederick Andrew, who took on the task of sifting through a huge compilation to help me choose the first twenty-five that I sent off for my original submission (It was not a thankless task, after all). Thank you to Jessica Kristie and Winter Goose Publishing for the belief in me, and James Koukis for all the commas.

Special acknowledgment and thanks go to my talented daughter, Olivia Ellen MacDonald, whose splendid photographs never cease to inspire me, some of which are included in this collection.

About the Author

Poet and writer Miriam Dunn grew up on the pristine shores of Cape Breton Island, with Canada's Atlantic coast and local woodlands as the inspiring backdrop to her life. Moved by her surroundings at a young age, her work is heavily influenced by the natural world, as well as human relationships. With a degree in Education, Miriam has been a web-writer for many years and her poetry and prose has appeared in numerous anthologies.

www.ingramcontent.com/pod-product-compliance
Lightning Source LLC
Chambersburg PA
CBHW051346040426
42453CB00007B/428